SHINE

Books by Joseph Millar

Overtime
Fortune
Blue Rust
Kingdom
Dark Harvest
Shine

SHINE

JOSEPH MILLAR

Carnegie Mellon University Press
Pittsburgh 2024

Acknowledgments

Many thanks to the editors of journals in which these poems appeared:

Alaska Quarterly Review: "Twilight," "Home"
American Poetry Review: "Cinematography," "Hymn," "Materials"
Catamaran: "Inward"
Chicago Review: "June Weddings"
Cholla Needles: "Upon Waking," "'Underledge'"
Five Points: "Wildfire Season," "The Sacred Altar of Poetry," "Shine,"
    "December 21"
Harvard Review: "Racetrack"
Plume: "Immersive," "New Year's Testament," "Eclipse 2," "Bed," "She"
Poetry: "Ars Poetica 3"
Prairie Schooner: "Ars Poetica 2," "Blessed with Work," "Dark Woods,"
    "For Annie 2," "Elegiacal," "Swan Song"
Raleigh Review: "Apollinaire"
San Pedro River Review: "Director's Cut"

"Planet Labor" also appeared in *What Things Cost, an anthology for the people,*
edited by Rebecca Gayle Howell and Ashley M. Jones, University of Kentucky
Press, 2023.

"Yet" also appeared in the anthology *Nickel*, edited by Vaughan Fielder, Weight of
Bees Press, 2022.

Special thanks to Monday Poetry: Sharon Olds, Matthew Dickman, Major and
Didi Jackson, Mike McGriff and Dorianne Laux. Thanks to Heather Bowlan.
Thanks as always to the best: Gerald Costanzo, Cynthia Lamb and Connie
Amoroso. Thanks to Pacific University's MFA and to Jeff Walt and the Desert Rat
Writer's Residency. Thanks above all to John-Roger: "Not one soul will be lost."

Book design by Anna Cappella

for Sharon Olds

"Tyger, Tyger burning bright"

—*William Blake*

Clang

"To give out a loud, resonant sound, as that produced by a large bell or two heavy pieces of metal striking together."

www.dictionary.com

CONTENTS

HANDS

The secrets of hands
fallen in ruin, knuckles
collapsing under pocked skin,
tendons aching, the body's rust,
though you have certainly
not grown thin.
Years ago you liked to come home
in the midnight hour
carrying suitcase and beer
and dragging the ghost of your mother
aloft in the wings of her hair.

And no one remembers the cold that returns
like a silent wing over the roof
the cypress and the camelia
where the doves take turns
in the darkened leaves
under your laundry room window
sitting on their two eggs
listening to the rinse and flush
empty itself to the dregs.

And walking around in your stocking feet
you start acting like someone's mother:
watering the spider fern and the pothos,
washing the glasses and pan.
Then turning off all the lights,
lights in the kitchen over the stove
flickering over your hands:
the crease in the palm,

the hand of fate, the hand of kindness
holding the gate
open at least partway—
lifeline and the heartline
sunk in deeper each day.

MATERIALS

There are pieces of silver and pieces of rock,
wood blades spinning in the ceiling fan,
the temperature's high, maybe over a hundred

where you sleep in the electric TV light
with the clicker under your hand
and when I was a boy, I slept in the attic
next to my pagan drum

though sometimes I felt like an alien there,
rhythmic and speechless, partly ashamed
and I dreamed of a woman with wine-colored hair
swirled back like a mane.

Today I know there's no God but God
watching the big woman next door
bending down in her purple robe
and putting out food for the cats

for she must have been in love before
standing outside in the shadows alone
listening to gulls cry out in the wind

which goes wherever it wants to go
and may not return again.

PLANET LABOR

I should be letting the sunlight
lead me into the darkness today
as my friend likes to say
speaking of jazz
or at least trying to fix the latch
on the front door
beyond which the sprinkler
rains down on the clover the old man,
my neighbor, plants for his bees,
whose honey I harvested yesterday
in a festival fraught with humming and death
garbed in my white jacket and mask
from the Yemeni beekeeper in Oakland
who lets them walk on his face and his neck.

For they are the hardest workers on earth
with their gold fur and leg hairs
packed with pollen, their long proboscises
filling with nectar,
then flying miles to the hive.

Now the sun has come out
over the hive's vast female
multiplicity, its center the darkened cells
of the brood and the queen who can live
for up to six years laying thousands
of eggs each day, her sireless drones
mostly useless now, pushed out to the edge
or driven away.

It's a hollow tree or maybe a box
made out of wood and wire
and any hard worker can tell you
there's nothing too restful about desire.
If you wanted to sleep
you should have stayed home,
in less than two months
your wings will be gone,
tattered from flying and fanning the air
to cool off the hive
and protect the brood,
they can look for you
lying still on the ground,
your work blooming everywhere.

RACETRACK

for Grew

We didn't come just for money and chance
for we like to gaze at the horses
being saddled now
for the 31st running of the Gold Rush Stakes,
the pale straw scattered underfoot
and the jockeys with Spanish names
climbing into the irons.
You sit here talking out loud
to nobody
penciling up the Form
in a threadbare sweater and Giants cap
deliberating some arcane combination,
your infected foot wrapped in gauze,
four twenties still left in your pocket
from a winner in the fourth.

Let's just stay here and never go back
jittering around in the betting line
trying to keep an eye on the chalk:
the infield grass metallic gray,
the sea turning bright, then dark.
There's a clutch of paper roses taped
to the mirror behind the bar,
a big cup filled with gold beer
and a southbound train in the distance
with a fat man ordering up the big lunch
behind the dining car's plate glass window
which glows like platinum or seawater
under the cut sun of March.

THE WOMEN OF RAIN

Let us not think of death or paradise
as the rainclouds come close
over Contra Costa County
and the darkness falls on the plain.
Let the women of rain come stepping down,
for they know what to expect
with their long skirts and fine hands,
their hair like smoke and their sunglasses
shining like lakes in the sand.

They will take time to talk and laugh,
they already have tickets and a backstage pass
and their voices overflow
with many inflections
as they watch the cumulus pile up in the north,
shaped like a rosebush or a placenta,
silver with ice heading west to the mountains.
You set out to find a barometer-reading
watching the wind blow a plastic bag
into the cyclone fence near the tracks
but the women of rain don't worry about it
for even if you return empty-handed
they know you're coming back.

MARRIOTT TAMPA

I've tried to leave the TV behind,
to renounce the clamor
of the Golden Globes
and also the amnesiac tones
beloved by my wife
of the *Unsolved Mysteries* series:
murder most foul, as the man has said,
the bones of a young woman
long since dead
dug up in a marsh outside Tampa
where the ibis birds
with their curved beaks
still pick their way through the hotel lawn
and the bay light settles
on sawblade palmetto leaves
next to the boulevard at dawn
where they sell more painkillers
than anywhere
north of the border—
even more than the mountains
of West Virginia.
On one side, the world
in its waking dream,
on the other, the soft waves
of endless sleep
which are slowly stealing the land away
in the cold silence between.

STOMACHACHE

Today the doctor herself got sick
and cancelled our appointment,

the Indian doctor with a Venetian broach
pinned to her Ivy League blouse

hand-carved from dark jade
and shaped like a turtle

perhaps to remind herself of the earth,
while she paces the bleached hallways of science

her white lab coat hanging now
where she left it, her stethoscope

and blood pressure gauge,
the ceiling tiles crisscrossed

with low-voltage wires
feeding the stuttering screens.

Maybe it's this humid weather
making everyone sick.

My wife bleats softly bending down
taking her robe from the dryer.

She moans to herself on the sofa
looking out at the fireflies of August

blinking over the narrow road,
black as a hearse, black as a river.

Maybe it's the stomach where memory lives
or maybe it's in the liver.

VISIT

In between gusts of chronic March wind
like some great migrant bird, the kind
that can navigate in the dark,
my oldest returns
trailing threads of the past
and carrying his present-day burdens here
from the first to the last.

Was he six when we rode
the old carousel, Saturdays in the park?
He's the reason the draft board
left me alone in the days
Vietnam raged and burned,
body count each night on the news,
babies still being born.
We made nicknames for each other then:
Catfish and *Parkside*, as though
we were making a story to save
for the years apart, when he deserved
so much more than I gave.

Today's early light like woven gauze
lies on his face where he sleeps,
the fears of the day erased for now:
the prices of everything, war in Ukraine,
finding a home in this US life
close enough to the Buddha
for his Vietnamese bride and my grandson . . .
he's breathing deep in the narrow room,
the bed too small for his frame.

DIRECTOR'S CUT

Because today Dennis Hopper's gone,
dead from a metastasized prostate

which he suffered as long as he could,
leaving his Rauschenbergs and his Warhols,

his painter's eye and his Nikon
which he could never escape

having now left behind Venice's streets,
a series of roles he didn't admire . . .

though if there's another sky beyond this one
fractured with copper light,

surely its moon shines on the hotel
where the hit man he played in *Backtrack*,

keeps practicing the saxophone—
as though he's decided art must be

the last refuge for someone like him:
the uncropped photographs, black-and-white

framed in Mexican tin, the collages and
silver gelatin prints, and the wings

of the death moth following him
all the last ten years of his life

darkly forged into jewelry.

AMENDS

What belongs to you this afternoon
as the novocaine wears off
is mostly the fine September dust
the color of honey drifted there
along the swash
at the field's edge
which the worms have collected
and left behind,
particles of Eden deposited
beneath the scarecrow with his sewn mouth
who can't feel his face or eyes
and not the least part of his painted tongue
though he's forgotten his hunger
for pills and booze
and he doesn't get headaches
listening to the news.
His silence becomes him like the air
that smells of leaf-smoke and sunscreen
as if he knows there's nothing to say
that will make things right again.

ARS POETICA

Why must you try to penetrate the silence
since you can never speak what is?

Why can't you stay in the small room,
why can't you shut the door?

Instead you sneak down early
and hover outside the retreat-grounds kitchen

where the cooks are yelling at the World Cup—
Argentina two-zip over France—

and out here in the lobby
the fire is snapping the pine logs

small explosions the tenor of laughter:
a shapely fire like a rosebush

unfolding behind its granite hearth
scattering its petals, flower by flower

where you linger alone
bereft of sleep, trying

to hold your attention still,
no longer needing to speak.

NEW YEAR'S TESTAMENT

The naked streets are running with rain,
the iron manhole lid on the sewer

bubbling up like a jukebox
and you're stepping over cypress roots

knobbed and yellow sticking out of the mud.

Last night's spasms of melancholy,
auld lang syne notwithstanding

like some secondary form of narcissism,
maybe it's in the blood.

So much unconscious freight
you want to lighten the load

for the world today doesn't seem old

and no matter whose calloused hands
will one day be digging your grave,

you're trying to leave enough in the pot
to make sure the digger gets paid.

TWILIGHT

Sometimes I think you'd give anything
to disappear into the twilight again
to walk ashore, not looking back

through the forest's insomniac shuffling,
ravens loosening their wings in the pines
where the dry ferns crackle under your soles.

In your left hand a glass of yellow wine
which glows like a blurry lens
through the dusky air from counties east

smelling of burning grass
and it's not like we're lost in these woods,
having drifted through here before

for our life together seems like a river
and your hair a world full of time and despair
which I can't compare to any other

its red thickness streaked with gray—
you with your perfumes and me with my feathers:
we were never delicate lovers.

OUTSIDE SACRAMENTO

In this version of the afterlife
let her relax in a cotton shirt
after the simple, delicate lunch
and let the man in the kitchen
cleaning the steel pans and stove
who has loved her all his life
finish his meticulous work.
He has a pain in his shoulder
in this version of the afterlife
from holding her all night long
in the scattered, half-unpacked rooms
nearby where the trees in the yard,
the apples and figs and plums
all need water
and the sky is gray with smoke.
The wind in the yellow fields keeps on
rustling the furry, desiccated husks
and online they study their Hindu texts
till she takes a nap on her left side
which is slowly going numb.
In this version of the afterlife
the Chinese landlord's property agent
has finally got them a new air conditioner
so they can rest in the coolness together
vulnerable and invincible
under the desert stars.

BLESSED WITH WORK

It went okay, trimming the bushes
growing over the back porch and stairs
of the house where my brother's widow
resides, the mimosa and ivy
he left behind, thin rain
spattering the windows nearby.
It can feel hopeless, being somebody's father
but it's all right being somebody's brother
for brothers are born and they rise up in time
and sometimes they never learn to sing
though on a day like this in the early spring
we were blessed with work, which we loved
together, like roots in the backyard dirt.
They keep pushing deeper and farther below
where the sun doesn't reach and the light doesn't show
but the roots never mind,
they never left Eden,
they think of work as a second heaven.
Their eye is single,
they think without words,
they don't need a gun and they don't
need a sword.

CINEMATOGRAPHY

Before you were born the wily sphinx
with its wide-open busted face and eye
rose high over the desert land,
Father of Dread with its lion's body
posing its riddle
on the nature of man—
and the same wind blowing
over the estuary, blowing open our door,
barging right in like it owns the place
as my wife likes to say
cursing quietly to herself:
gale warnings posted all afternoon
gusting suddenly, then shifting away
in its rampant, ruthless joy
and feeling it, my youngest began to run,
oddly balanced on his stroke-numbed leg.
He ran by himself in the open field
leaning forward and free,
a short dash to the fence and then again,
filming himself with his cell phone
which twinkled in the grass like an insect,
for as Meister Eckhardt has said,
"The same eye with which I see God
is the eye with which God sees me."

FOR ANNIE 2

All afternoon the west wind
has been blowing its heavy gusts

bending the elm and alder branches
over the clover and fescue grass

where we watched the two snakes
entwine and mate

like the strands
of a high-voltage cable.

If you left me
where could I go in this world

and not feel like a stranger?
World of mourning

things left behind, of turning around
and not going back.

I waited two hours in Emoryville
keeping watch over the tracks

till you finally stepped from
the southbound Coast Starlight

carrying the same small notebook
all the way down from Oregon,

wishing you had a cigarette
and holding the damp green skin of night

darkly against your body.

SHINE

The fire burns down against the rocks
turning the ashes white
and the petals of the Christmas flower
open their points out
like a new star
which the world is making
every moment,
making new stars day and night.
In the pale grass
and brown straw fallen
under the cypress and pines,
new stars being made
so common and rare
burning away in the desert air
where sometimes the wind
makes a sound like a flute
and only the wild things set foot.
They shine on the ice fields in the far north
and all through heaven and earth.
There are piles of dark kelp
washed up in the sand,
washed in the fullness of time
and the moon's a bright crescent
just past new
hanging above the waves
which are making new stars
in their spindrift and whitecaps
and making new stars in their depth,
new stars in the abysses and canyons
shining on life and death.

WHAT THE RIVER SAYS

for William Stafford

I believe whatever it tells me
in its low voice husky
with autumn, the earth's crust
broken open by water,
turquoise and pale or brown and yellow,
flowing northeast or southwest
stroking the sides of its bed,
then widening over the shoals
of gravel, ditch weed and mud.

I believe when it says
there's no ice to hold onto
where the equinox light
slips into the current
wide and sleepless
past swamps and peat grass, bridges
of steel, train yards, motel rooms
next to the beach
with an addict's corpse lying still
and the sirens coursing their way
through the night
most people look away from

and the world keeps flowing
downhill toward morning,
relentless, not stopping
each way we look, traveling
the black streets
of coffee and sugar
and everyone telling the time:
time forgotten, time to go,
Whitman's multitudes, earthbound, striving,
fused with his neural, electric substance,

river of phosphorous, silicates, manganese,
iron that came from the stars—
river you can't step into twice
that there's no escaping for good,
copper and salt and selenium
lighting up in the blood.

SKYDIVER FROM SPACE

*for Felix Baumgartner, daredevil stuntman who
sky dived from 24 miles in the stratosphere,
reaching speeds of over 840 mph, October 14, 2012.*

Yours is the night no one sleeps in
nameless and freezing
though the fire of stars
flickers above the rim of the world,
and the darkness
leans its head on your chest
when you step from the capsule
in your bone-white suit
filled with oxygen
and sewn up with mirrors,
its cameras floating in nitrogen,
their housings strapped to your sleeves,
free-falling, shining down
through the cold dark
faster than sound
into the lit blue
New Mexican sky
where your chute finally opens
like a giant flower
into the warm thick air
and no one else
sees the desert floor
rising to meet you, floating slow
over Roswell and Area 51,
the ghosts of old UFOs,
the ghosts of Mescalero Apache—
not to mention the earth's very own
agave and sagebrush, false indigo,
spiny and thin in its limestone crevices
shining up from the gypsum below.

WILDFIRE SEASON

She wants you to follow the tracks to the sea
and stop thinking about tomorrow,
the tracks of the ravens, herons and crows
that scar up the landscape
and keep pressing down,
and though you don't wish
to go through this again
she wants you to rise up into the air
with its smoke and particles falling like rain,
ashes of trees and houses and cars,
burned-up vineyards, burned-up guitars,
even the ashes of someone's mother
shaped like a little French wing,
an aileron hovering above California
where the trains roll south
and the crossing bells ring,
for these are the days to be patient
and try not to want anything
and these are the nights
you can't see the stars,
to drink extra water
and climb the stairs slowly
and practice your quietest breathing.

MENDOCINO PERSEIDS

It should be easy to read in this bed
with its slanted wood headboard
made for sitting up,
this day having passed in tranquility
though the Café Beaujolais
is now owned by a Mexican
so the lamb barbacoa is excellent
and no more coq au vin

for the retirees who line up outside
to sample the five-star takeout
during this summer of Covid
in their windbreakers from LL Bean,
and if I am not one of them
I am nothing:
the same crepe skin, the same tired breath
of sighs and gossip and rust—
many desires grown abstract and vague,
rain on the sea at dusk.

I think of the rivers of Babylon
where the people sat down and wept
and the pain where my left leg
which keeps getting older
joins onto the rest of my hip
and the many times words fail me
when the wind moans through the leaves,
a disheveled chanteuse that can't get to sleep,
her back aches and so do her knees
under the asteroid metal fires
that come burning out of the past,
they call them the tears of St. Laurence,
broken off from their comet and left behind
and turning to blowing ash.

JUNE WEDDINGS

Suppose the virus was spreading out
over the heaving lungs of the South
and suppose the store
where they sell wedding gowns
stayed open during the quarantine,
its arched backdoor agape like a mouth
that's not afraid to be infected,
the gowns floating like solitary clouds
behind the shimmering glass
and the planet holding so still right now
I would hate to leave it,
never having seen you in such a dress
though married these many years . . .

I watch you lean over the flower bed
listening to something in the afternoon wind
under the big eucalyptus
and leaving the rest of the world behind—
wherever you are, in whatever time—
for beauty will never apologize
for the trouble it's caused in everyone's lives—
whatever it owes to the roses and moon,
or the volcanoes under the sea
the sound of bells or an old country tune
before the season is done.

WAITING ON THE POEM

Sometimes when I'm writing
I like to sit up straight in the quiet
imagining a large rhododendron plant

like the ones that grow in Oregon
pushing its blue flowers out
over our backyard thistles and dandelions

where the crows will gather for decades to come
to violate the stillness
with their sudden voices

waiting to be fed peanuts in the shell
at the hand of my wife—
next to the broken stairs

and sometimes I think of the Arab forms,
and the troubadours of Provence,
Arnaut Daniel and Bernard de Ventadour

composing for the unattainable muse,
some distant sideways lady of the castle—
Eleanor of Aquitaine, Margaret de Turenne—

sestina and aubade
in their rhythms and stress—
vernacular music passed down the line—

it's a long time till it gets here
to you and me, little voice.

HYMN

Sometimes I imagine the good life
as a salad of celery and iceberg lettuce,
and a big chunk of homemade bread
tasting faintly of salt
and in my blue cup, shining brightly up
the light-roast coffee from Ethiopia
with the ivory rain falling outside
over the shorn earth of California
and its dark railroad tracks,
their cinders and Queen Anne's lace—
and then I imagine the long train
passing over the threshold to Southern Cal
blasting its whistle along through the mountains
and the twisting arms of the Joshua trees
down through the desert sand
with its cholla needles and creosote
and the fibrous blades of the agave,
which, it turns out, is a type of asparagus
the Mexicans use to make sandals and rope
and sometimes cook down into honey,
world without end, amen.

INWARD

It's five in the afternoon
and you let the silence

come present,
its shadow that fills you up.

No more climbing the big rock
high above Lighthouse Beach,

no more chaining line on the ice
over the Beaufort Sea.

For you loved the white box cake she baked
in a glass dish shaped like a dome

its edges were burned and they tasted good
though they had no nutritional value

and these are the days you mostly stay home.
Even so, the air can vibrate

blowing over some western hill
while you keep watch toward the waterfall

where it looks like the land is moving
and the river is standing still.

BREATH

She was talking about the blind masseuse
digging gently into the muscles
either side of her spine,
the bamboo plant and the rain outdoors
and the guide dog asleep in the corner
sighing in time
with her groans of release,
her forehead held by the little wood gutter,
tears coming out of her eyes, spellbound
and falling a great long distance,
maybe twelve storeys down.

In the book on the Tao my friend gave me
Chuang Tzu speaks of a huge fish
with trillions of scales
alluvial and celestial,
too many to count and far too long
from its eyes to the fin of its tail,
allegria and adagio,
and a giant bird as well.
It wasn't that much about heaven and hell,
no false star to follow, just a deep breath
into the lungs and into the blood
to light up the trillions of cells.

ECLIPSE 2

You would get used to it after a while,
the least sound of the gondola cars

shimmying down the tracks.
Coal dust on the sills

and inkblot bird's feet
randomly walking there—

desolate hills near the river.
Your long shadow keeps hiding the stars

where you've gone unconscious
and forgotten the ones

you were supposed to speak to tonight
in the olive grove of Zoom TV

with its mute ripples of blue and green:
the post office closed, the racetrack closed,

all the houseboats tilted aground
and the moon in full eclipse,

somewhat like your daughter at four
in the days before you stopped drinking

covering your eyes with her small hands
and telling you to guess who it is.

YET

I've already forgotten the words,
something about a nickel, something
about a candle gone out,
the indigo loveliness of November,
blackberry canes grown down close to the path
and the monarch butterflies gathered in throngs
in the deep woods of Michoacán.
The honeybees cluster
around the brood combs
keeping the future alive
and surely we shall all meet again
somewhere up in the Great Northwest
as if we remembered the passage back
to where we drank the dark boundless air
and saw the stars melt in the river
and learned to follow our breath.

DARK WOODS

There's no one in the forest to help you
with the task of remembering your name

no secret ceremony in the leaves
this far away from home

with a sound in your ears like tinnitus,
a distant ringing from outer space

or it could be water running over the stones
of a woman's backbone, away from her face.

Oh bride of science called down from the stars,
oh glass jar placed on a hill

to focus the mind in its ranging flight
over the ragged wilderness
and the ocean that looks like wrecked steel.

This time of life can make its own weather
and sometimes bring its own fear

like the dry wind blowing west from Nevada
threatening the land with fire.

But you know you want to give something back
to the woods which have held you

when you lay down to sleep
below the ledges of rock and the oaks

their limbs stretched out through the smoke of November,
their roots sunk vast and deep.

ELEGIACAL

To keep from feeling abandoned by beauty
you open the poems of James Schuyler

with their sleeping pills and cologne—
raspberries gathered in an amethyst wine glass

and the dresses in the Fashion Institute,
"celadon lined with jade."

You forget the fires burning in Yosemite
and the rest of the planet suffering heat stroke

and turn on the TV to Harry Belafonte
speaking about the great Bill Russell—

he of the cat-moves around the rim, the deft
shot-blocking leaps

over 22 rebounds a game
and 11 championship rings—

who made the world call him a man first
and a basketball player second.

To keep from feeling abandoned by death
which by now has claimed both of them,

you think of the marine layer settling down
and the cold upwelling of seawater

giving rise to the anchovy bloom.

HOME

for Atchison Village

Under this roof when it was new
they got up early and came home late
from the shipyards during the war,
putting in seven twelves a week,
falling asleep in the car.
No one was watching the moon
from their bed
though it's new tonight,
too dark to see
and extra close to the earth:
dead low tide in the salt marsh
next to the bay and the racetrack—
where the lone egret roosts on saw grass
and a clump of tidal mud.
He's facing away from the chilly wind
and the freight train's whistle
bound for Los Angeles,
everything haunted the way we like it,
everything closing in.

BED

There's mist coming in from the west
and the black streets are shiny
passing St John's apartments
and covering the April palm trees
which are drunk and walking
in our village alleys.
Instead of the freight cars' heavy metal,
instead of the witch's hair,
instead of the fog horn's split bass tone
like a whale's heart
beating somewhere offshore,
it's the rain
someone anonymous longs for
in the small poem
falling softly all morning
onto the land and the old man's mattress
where he spent his final days
now stashed in the open truck
to be hauled away to the Richmond dump
for it's hard to say goodbye to a bed
with its shadows and tarnished frame
and wishing your love were back in your arms
among the soft breezes of spring.

VOTING RIGHTS

for John R. Lewis

I said goodbye and looked away
from the big ships unloading crude oil
from their steel tanks at the end of day
and the president's orange face on TV
standing in front of the titans of finance.
I was hoping they knew the plain laws of science
with the world locked down, staying inside
and the day coming on, no place to hide
from the sound of the cock
crowing at dawn,
from the pale light of the summer moon
and the people's heart keeping on.

I used to drink coffee and talk to my brother,
who I loved for the way he could take things apart
and also put them together
though his thinking continually veered to the left
no matter the season or weather.
We sang of the cowboy shot in the breast
walking out in the streets of Laredo,
we sang of the gray Irish mare of death,
the heralds of César Vallejo

and the bold young man who laced up his shoes
and stepped out onto the bridge
and wouldn't let anyone
turn him around,
for Medgar Evers and Martin King
for such is the spirit of life and breath
and such are the fathers of happiness.

SWAN SONG

You are like a swan with a broken wing,
Ophelia gliding through mansions of water
smelling the hesitant perfumes of night,
fig and skunk cabbage, railroad flowers,
shells washed up in the campfire light.
We think of her down there under the current,
who my friend says is a Christ figure
weighed down by betrayal and grief
and her long clothes and her chevelure,
whose mother we never meet.

And listening to jazz
in Sam's Park Place Barber Shop
where I've paid for the first shave of my life
lying back at age 78,
coconut oil and my face in a hot towel
only my nose sticking out
like a gangster boss in a film noir,
the low-down blues stalking around
Jimmy Smith and Stanley Turrentine.
Alas poor Cannonball I knew him well
who winked at me climbing onto the stage
in Baltimore's Famous Ballroom
winter of 1969,
another lord gone in the dark soil of history
or maybe it's really an ocean,
another lord surging into the tide
on the long wave of resurrection.

BAT MITZVAH

I don't know when I'm coming home
but I hope it's soon

walking in the dark this evening
with the Hudson gurgling under its piers,

part saltwater, part snowmelt
and hidden springs to the north,

a spring rain falling black and cold—
unknown, historical

like the streets of New York
or the Hebrew words memorized

by my granddaughter
to welcome her into adulthood.

Amos, the herdsman prophet
raising hell with the Jews

for not taking care of the poor—
the certainty of the desolation,

earthquake and fire on Samaria and Bethel
before the promise renews—

and meanwhile the river moves on its bed
not so far to the sea:

Welcome to adulthood, little Nadine.

APOLLINAIRE

We listen to the two-tone sirens
sounding their cry
maybe chasing a thief

like Honore Pieret, who slept on your couch
where he stashed the Egyptian statue

he stole from the Louvre
so you got busted and they took you downtown . . .
with your large eyes and small moustache

your overcoat and the headwound
you brought back from World War One
your tombstone with its heart-shaped poem

your mother's gambling addiction
your father entirely unknown,
your fine poem "Zone."

Maybe kindness is a sunny room,
someone looking out from its doorframe
through the city's trees and cement—

like you who invented the term surrealism
to describe the music of Erik Satie
and loved the grace of industrial streets:

the rooftops and metal, glass and smoke,
who saw like your friends Picasso and Braque
the different angles of being

the cubist cones and jagged planes
like crystal formations stacked and locked
deep in the optical brain.

ARS POETICA 2

I take out the trash in the rain
which glimmers here, a watery blur,

and murmurs aloud on the hoods of the cars
and rattles the garbage cans

for I provide room service on the first floor,
just leave the leftovers outside the door,

orange peels, half a scrambled egg,
splash of salsa left in the pan.

I have nothing to worry about, though I still do—
nor does my old neighbor, sprawled in his bunk

listening to rain in the cave of his room.
He's lame from arthritis but he's not drunk

though he misses the days of work,
his plasterer's trade with its trowels and knives

still tucked away under the eaves.
For breakfast I bring him a strawberry Ensure

until he can make it down the stairs
and roll the walker across to his chair

for coffee and toast with three or four prunes,
and a program about fishing in the Tasman Sea

smoking his long pipe of Turkish tobacco,
or he might call his daughter in Indiana

though inside of me and inside of him
there's a white shark that never rests—

it swims all night through the stomach and heart
like the ceaseless, predatory mind of art.

AUTUMN

In the Piedmont the soft night keeps falling
gently onto the plain
and we are so late for the rehearsal dinner
I know we'll miss it for sure,
with its hubbub of voices raised on high
in the promise of wedding toasts
though out here the white roses of frost
keep chafing the October roadside,
the sounds of a foghorn, sounds of the sea
coming toward us over the field.

Tonight we are free from the burdens
of childhood, the full moon's scarred
and anonymous shadows
and we are not sorry for the life
we have led—newspaper, suitcase, hotel coffee—
holding hands in the front seat
breathing the cold air
that smells of salt
in this country without a name.

DECEMBER 21

This year an old guy named Lewis
has driven me to the market
in his ancient blue half-ton Ford
which goes by the name of Anthony
and has a hole in the floor
and we've loaded up with a Christmas ham
and spinach and twelve ruby-skin yams,
pumpkin filling in an oversized can,
cinnamon sticks from Vietnam
and one copy of *USA Today*,
useless except for the crossword
for today is the winter solstice,
winter to half the earth,
shortest day, longest night
here in the quiet north
under the moon and Venus above,
Saturn conjunct with Jupiter
where no one needs to anxiously hope
or endlessly seek for love
though we can write down a solstice wish
and throw it into the fire
and peel an orange in the darkness.

ARS POETICA 3

Your friends tell you the writing
is good but you're not actually buying it—
so much idle conversation, you think,
overheard through a hotel window
by a cab driver half asleep in the sun
instead of an ode or a psalm—

and waiting near the ER for your wife
who has just broken her arm,
reading a translation of Hafez or Tagore
can make you feel godless and small
since you're not Neil Young or François Villon
though on such a day or night as this
you hear the footsteps along the sidewalk
and here comes the old shadow again
like the promise of late-season rain
which you hope will keep falling
into the earth, its rivers and deserts,
its alleys and streets
and the wild wastrel ocean.

SPLENDOR

Something about the horses walking
approaching the gate for the Belmont Stakes,
their closeness and warmth—
each sandy hoof—
because the real self is sincere
delighting in the jockeys' bright silks,
and in love with the air
though wondering perhaps
about the nature of thought
as opposed to say, mentalizing
which tries to make mental
what remains unknown.

Someone kiss Daniel, kiss Annie too
and Tristem and Peggy and Joe—
come in here and kiss us all, one by one.
Give us a nice big kiss and a poem
to be read to the walls of the mind
like the huge asteroid, half a mile wide
and 12 times the height of the Empire State Building
passing close to the earth
or the brown rabbit eating a strawberry
crouched there among the lilies.

SHE

She's changing the sheets in the room above,
the dew settling onto the windowsill
and onto the scarlet bougainvillea
smudged with coal dust and smoke.
Sometimes I hear her long sigh on the stairs
and if I want to listen, I must be quiet,
I have to disappear.

Sometimes the damp earth of the cemetery
gives off the fragrance of pears,
sometimes the ferns' eyelash lacework
floats through our dense marine layer
and if I were a woman
I'd make my bed there
where I could see the moon
and maybe I'd wear a blue housedress,
the only thing holding me to the earth.

UPON WAKING

Upon waking, the flat, silent realm
where you were traveling
and refining your earthly lessons
pulls back too far to recall very much:
spoon-feeding scrambled eggs
to a two-year-old,
watching your wife lean back in the sand.

It could be any street
running down to the sea,
anyone's busted skiff in the backyard
planted with beans and roses
watching her lovely, naked feet
crossed over and resting
silently there
and the long waves
rustling salt hay up the beach
into a long, crooked line—

every hair on the grandchildren's heads
numbered and dear to God,
though behind you there's 100 miles of bad road,
meteor showers and hurricanes, history
being made every day,
poetry and some kind of silence
you would not betray.

"UNDERLEDGE"

I stand and listen in the patch of wild grass
we called the Upper Meadow
surrounded by outcrops of New England granite
forced up from the ancient ground,
half bewitched by the murmur of bees
in the ragged October garden,
its tattered flags and disappearing pollen,
the dark honey of fall.
I hope we sell our father's house
with its musty stairs and brown shingles,
and the sea kayak perched in the rafters.
I'm hoping we sell the wisteria
growing across the arbor
not to mention the small upstairs room
with the dead fireplace
where I lay one winter, sick with the flu
looking out at the snow on the rock.
I hope we sell the siding and doors,
the hot water pipes running under the floor,
the hand-painted hex sign from Pennsylvania,
and the big window keeping watch on the sparrows
in their late-winter mania.
We could sell the air, smelling of cornbread,
smelling of chili and beer, the sound
of the night wind on the cove
howling over the beaches and river,
the silences after it passes on,
the stars and the moon's slow merry-go-round
under the patchwork heaven.

THE SACRED ALTAR OF POETRY

I like the night above the valley
where the snow would pile up in winter
and you could hear the crossing bells
of the long trains heading west.
I like the wee small hours of the morning
as Frank Sinatra would say
before the dawn slowly opens
into the silence of day.

Silence, the wellspring of happiness
which I won't raise my voice against,
my voice like a small twin-engine plane
lost in a cloud with no instruments.
At twilight I walk through the streets of town
through the wildfire smoke that kills all the smells,
horchata and masa and guacamole,
when I looked through the windows of tarnished glass
trying to buy headache pills.
Each night after supper I take out the trash
instead of making a song or an ode—
I wash the dishes, wipe down the stove:
if the muse were a whore, I'd give her the cash.

DOG DAYS

I will miss this dim house in the South
beneath the blades of the ceiling fan
where the air smells dense
and laced with must
the petals on the blue vase
speckled with rust,
fluted crown moldings over the bed
off-white curtains with dusty threads
and the mail piling up and the gray rain
falling outside on the cars
airplane tickets and wedding vows,
chicken and waffles, blackened fish,
the distant lust of the troubadours.

I'll miss the studio in back
with its lines of Faulkner's handwriting
praising the spirit of autumn
in a photocopy tacked to the wall,
patches of feathery mold once more
sanded away from the sills.

And sometimes I want the shadows
never to come to an end
crouched on the stairs and writing
with an aluminum fountain pen
in the days after Hurricane Florence
when the moon finally came back again,
shining down on the broken trees
the pine straw and ruined camelias,
the tombstone garbage cans in the alley,
the glare of the neighbor's TV.

It feels like I'm pawning an heirloom
which never belonged to me:
I stay home washing carrots and celery
and the fluted leaves of romaine,
then holding my hands out over the sink
empty and almost clean.

And it will be hard to leave behind
the cypress tree in the quiet before dawn
each time I wipe down the stove's
smudged burners, drinking water alone
and listening to the songbirds waken
long before night has gone.

IMMERSIVE

I meant to be talking of the huge cargo ship
jammed in the throat of the Suez Canal
which the full moon's tide
lifted free this morning
and also the spring's rare butterflies
jagging along the back fence
and my neighbor's accordian music
seething under the door
and the ways I can't pay attention for long
and the value of common sense—

I meant to be talking of Vincent Van Gogh
and the chipped light of wheat fields
he carried inside him
breaking apart in the noonday sun
the black wings of crows and the wreckage
of shadows, an old wagon
on fire in the ditch
or the eaves of a barn, its haymow
broken in half by time and the rain
falling on San Francisco
and the blue pigeon standing alone
under the tiny awning
where my love and I also stood
watching it come down like mercy,
like threads from some astral wardrobe
across from the old Fillmore West
drinking takeout coffee from the little kitchen
and waiting for the movie to start.

Notes

"Racetrack" is for David Pettigrew.

"Director's Cut" is for David St John.

"Outside Sacramento" is for Alan Jewett and Joan Holland.

"Shine" is for John Morton.

"What the River Says" is for William Stafford.

"Skydiver from Space" is for Felix Baumgartner.

"Bat Mitzvah" is for Nadine Schwartz.

"Voting Rights" is for Congressman John R. Lewis.

"Ars Poetica 2" is for Dale Turner.

"Breath" is for Laura Hendrie.

"'Underledge'" is for Jim Fastook, with apologies.